Key Facts™ on Thailand

~Essential Information on Thailand~

By Patrick W. Nee

The Internationalist®
www.internationalist.com

The Internationalist®
International Business, Investment, and Travel
Published by:
The Internationalist Publishing Company
96 Walter Street/ Suite 200
Boston, MA 02131, USA
Tel: 617-354-7722
www.internationalist.com
PN@internationalist.com

Copyright © 2014 by PWN

The Internationalist is a Registered Trademark. "Key Facts" and "The Internationalist Business Guides" are Trademarks of The Internationalist Publishing Company.

All Rights are reserved under International, Pan-American, and Pan-Asian Conventions. No part of this book may be reproduced in any form without the written permission of the publisher. All rights vigorously enforced

Table Of Contents

Chapter 1: Background

Chapter 2: Geography

Chapter 3: People and Society

Chapter 4: Government and Key Leaders

Chapter 5: Economy

Chapter 6: Energy

Chapter 7: Communications

Chapter 8: Transportation

Chapter 9: Military

Chapter 10: Transnational Issues

Map of Thailand

Chapter 1: Background

A unified Thai kingdom was established in the mid-14th century. Known as Siam until 1939, Thailand is the only Southeast Asian country never to have been taken over by a European power. A bloodless revolution in 1932 led to a constitutional monarchy. In alliance with Japan during World War II, Thailand became a US treaty ally in 1954 after sending troops to Korea and later fighting alongside the United States in Vietnam. Thailand since 2005 has experienced several rounds of political turmoil including a military coup in 2006 that ousted then Prime Minister THAKSIN Chinnawat, followed by large-scale street protests by competing political factions in 2008, 2009, and 2010. Demonstrations in 2010 culminated with clashes between security forces and pro-THAKSIN protesters, elements of which were armed, and resulted in at least 92 deaths and an estimated $1.5 billion in arson-related property losses. THAKSIN's youngest sister, YINGLAK Chinnawat, in 2011 led the Puea Thai Party to an electoral win and assumed control of the government. YINGLAK's leadership was almost immediately challenged by historic flooding in late 2011 that had large swathes of the country underwater and threatened to inundate Bangkok itself. Throughout 2012 the Puea Thai-led government struggled with the opposition Democrat Party to fulfill some of its main election promises, including constitutional reform and political reconciliation. Since January 2004, thousands have been killed and wounded in violence associated with the ethno-nationalist insurgency in Thailand's southern Malay-Muslim majority provinces.

Chapter 2: Geography

Location:
> Southeastern Asia, bordering the Andaman Sea and the Gulf of Thailand, southeast of Burma

Geographic coordinates:
> 15 00 N, 100 00 E

Map references:
> Southeast Asia

Area:
> total: 513,120 sq km
> country comparison to the world: 51
> land: 510,890 sq km
> water: 2,230 sq km

Area - comparative:
> slightly more than twice the size of Wyoming

Land boundaries:
> total: 4,863 km
> border countries: Burma 1,800 km, Cambodia 803 km, Laos 1,754 km, Malaysia 506 km

Coastline:
> 3,219 km

Maritime claims:
> territorial sea: 12 nm
> exclusive economic zone: 200 nm
> continental shelf: 200 m depth or to the depth of exploitation

Climate:
> tropical; rainy, warm, cloudy southwest monsoon (mid-May to September); dry, cool northeast monsoon (November to mid-March); southern isthmus always hot and humid

Terrain:
> central plain; Khorat Plateau in the east; mountains elsewhere

Elevation extremes:

lowest point: Gulf of Thailand 0 m

highest point: Doi Inthanon 2,576 m

Natural resources:

tin, rubber, natural gas, tungsten, tantalum, timber, lead, fish, gypsum, lignite, fluorite, arable land

Land use:

arable land: 30.71%

permanent crops: 8.77%

other: 60.52% (2011)

Irrigated land:

64,150 sq km (2007)

Total renewable water resources:

438.6 cu km (2011)

Freshwater withdrawal (domestic/industrial/agricultural):

total: 57.31 cu km/yr (5%/5%/90%)

per capita: 845.3 cu m/yr (2007)

Natural hazards:

land subsidence in Bangkok area resulting from the depletion of the water table; droughts

Environment - current issues:

air pollution from vehicle emissions; water pollution from organic and factory wastes; deforestation; soil erosion; wildlife populations threatened by illegal hunting

Environment - international agreements:

party to: Biodiversity, Climate Change, Climate Change-Kyoto Protocol, Desertification, Endangered Species, Hazardous Wastes, Marine Life Conservation, Ozone Layer Protection, Tropical Timber 83, Tropical Timber 94, Wetlands

signed, but not ratified: Law of the Sea

Geography - note:

controls only land route from Asia to Malaysia and Singapore

Chapter 3: People and Society

Nationality:
>noun: Thai (singular and plural)
>adjective: Thai

Ethnic groups:
>Thai 75%, Chinese 14%, other 11%

Languages:
>Thai, English (secondary language of the elite), ethnic and regional dialects

Religions:
>Buddhist (official) 94.6%, Muslim 4.6%, Christian 0.7%, other 0.1% (2000 census)

Population:
>67,448,120 (July 2013 est.)
>
>country comparison to the world: 20
>
>note: estimates for this country explicitly take into account the effects of excess mortality due to AIDS; this can result in lower life expectancy, higher infant mortality, higher death rates, lower population growth rates, and changes in the distribution of population by age and sex than would otherwise be expected (July 2013 est.)

Age structure:
>0-14 years: 19.2% (male 6,620,873/female 6,313,188)
>15-24 years: 15.1% (male 5,181,468/female 4,975,083)
>25-54 years: 45.6% (male 15,192,334/female 15,569,761)
>55-64 years: 10.4% (male 3,345,493/female 3,661,867)
>65 years and over: 9.8% (male 2,971,426/female 3,616,627) (2013 est.)

Median age:
>total: 35.1 years
>male: 34.2 years
>female: 36.1 years (2013 est.)

Population growth rate:
>0.52% (2013 est.)
>
>country comparison to the world: 150

Birth rate:

    12.66 births/1,000 population (2013 est.)

    country comparison to the world: 156

Death rate:

    7.47 deaths/1,000 population (2013 est.)

    country comparison to the world: 115

Net migration rate:

    0 migrant(s)/1,000 population (2013 est.)

    country comparison to the world: 76

Urbanization:

    urban population: 34.1% of total population (2011)

    rate of urbanization: 1.6% annual rate of change (2010-15 est.)

Major urban areas - population:

    BANGKOK (capital) 6.902 million (2009)

Sex ratio:

    at birth: 1.05 male(s)/female

    0-14 years: 1.05 male(s)/female

    15-24 years: 1.04 male(s)/female

    25-54 years: 0.97 male(s)/female

    55-64 years: 0.92 male(s)/female

    65 years and over: 0.82 male(s)/female

    total population: 0.98 male(s)/female (2013 est.)

Maternal mortality rate:

    48 deaths/100,000 live births (2010)

    country comparison to the world: 110

Infant mortality rate:

    total: 15.41 deaths/1,000 live births

    country comparison to the world: 107

    male: 16.38 deaths/1,000 live births

    female: 14.39 deaths/1,000 live births (2013 est.)

Life expectancy at birth:

total population: 74.05 years

country comparison to the world: 115

male: 71.66 years

female: 76.58 years (2013 est.)

Total fertility rate:

1.66 children born/woman (2013 est.)

country comparison to the world: 175

Contraceptive prevalence rate:

79.6% (2009)

Health expenditures:

3.9% of GDP (2010)

country comparison to the world: 169

Physicians density:

0.3 physicians/1,000 population (2004)

Hospital bed density:

2.1 beds/1,000 population (2010)

Drinking water source:

improved:

urban: 97% of population

rural: 95% of population

total: 96% of population

unimproved:

urban: 3% of population

rural: 5% of population

total: 4% of population (2010 est.)

Sanitation facility access:

improved:

urban: 95% of population

rural: 96% of population

total: 96% of population

unimproved:

urban: 5% of population

rural: 4% of population

total: 4% of population (2010 est.)

HIV/AIDS - adult prevalence rate:

1.3% (2009 est.)

country comparison to the world: 38

HIV/AIDS - people living with HIV/AIDS:

530,000 (2009 est.)

country comparison to the world: 15

HIV/AIDS - deaths:

28,000 (2009 est.)

country comparison to the world: 13

Major infectious diseases:

degree of risk: very high

food or waterborne diseases: bacterial diarrhea

vectorborne diseases: dengue fever, Japanese encephalitis, and malaria

note: highly pathogenic H5N1 avian influenza has been identified in this country; it poses a negligible risk with extremely rare cases possible among US citizens who have close contact with birds (2013)

Obesity - adult prevalence rate:

8.8% (2008)

country comparison to the world: 135

Children under the age of 5 years underweight:

7% (2006)

country comparison to the world: 76

Education expenditures:

3.8% of GDP (2010)

country comparison to the world: 119

Literacy:

definition: age 15 and over can read and write

total population: 92.6%

male: 94.9%

female: 90.5% (2000 census)

School life expectancy (primary to tertiary education):

total: 12 years

male: 12 years

female: 13 years (2009)

Child labor - children ages 5-14:

total number: 818,399

percentage: 8 % (2006 est.)

Unemployment, youth ages 15-24:

total: 2.7%

country comparison to the world: 140

male: 2.5%

female: 3% (2011)

Mother's mean age at first birth:

23

note: Median age at first birth among women 25-29 (1987 est.)

Chapter 4: Government and Key Leaders

Country name:
>conventional long form: Kingdom of Thailand
>conventional short form: Thailand
>local long form: Ratcha Anachak Thai
>local short form: Prathet Thai
>former: Siam

Government type:
>constitutional monarchy

Capital:
>name: Bangkok
>geographic coordinates: 13 45 N, 100 31 E
>time difference: UTC+7 (12 hours ahead of Washington, DC during Standard Time)

Administrative divisions:
>77 provinces (changwat, singular and plural); Amnat Charoen, Ang Thong, Bueng Kan, Buriram, Chachoengsao, Chai Nat, Chaiyaphum, Chanthaburi, Chiang Mai, Chiang Rai, Chon Buri, Chumphon, Kalasin, Kamphaeng Phet, Kanchanaburi, Khon Kaen, Krabi, Krung Thep Mahanakhon (Bangkok), Lampang, Lamphun, Loei, Lop Buri, Mae Hong Son, Maha Sarakham, Mukdahan, Nakhon Nayok, Nakhon Pathom, Nakhon Phanom, Nakhon Ratchasima, Nakhon Sawan, Nakhon Si Thammarat, Nan, Narathiwat, Nong Bua Lamphu, Nong Khai, Nonthaburi, Pathum Thani, Pattani, Phangnga, Phatthalung, Phayao, Phetchabun, Phetchaburi, Phichit, Phitsanulok, Phra Nakhon Si Ayutthaya, Phrae, Phuket, Prachin Buri, Prachuap Khiri Khan, Ranong, Ratchaburi, Rayong, Roi Et, Sa Kaeo, Sakon Nakhon, Samut Prakan, Samut Sakhon, Samut Songkhram, Sara Buri, Satun, Sing Buri, Sisaket, Songkhla, Sukhothai, Suphan Buri, Surat Thani, Surin, Tak, Trang, Trat, Ubon Ratchathani, Udon Thani, Uthai Thani, Uttaradit, Yala, Yasothon

Independence:
>1238 (traditional founding date; never colonized)

National holiday:
>Birthday of King PHUMIPHON (BHUMIBOL), 5 December (1927)

Constitution:
24 August 2007

Legal system:
civil law system with common law influences

International law organization participation:
has not submitted an ICJ jurisdiction declaration; non-party state to the ICCt

Suffrage:
18 years of age; universal and compulsory

Executive branch:

chief of state: King PHUMIPHON Adunyadet, also spelled BHUMIBOL Adulyadej (since 9 June 1946)

head of government: Prime Minister YINGLAK Chinnawat also spelled YINGLUCK Shinawatra (since 8 August 2011); Deputy Prime Minister KITTIRAT Na Ranong (since 28 October 2012); Deputy Prime Minister PHONGTHEP Therkanchana also spelled PHONGTHEP Thepkanchana (since 28 October 2012); Deputy Prime Minister PLODPRASOP Suraswadi (since 28 October 2012); Deputy Prime Minister PRACHA Promnok (since 24 March 2013); Deputy Prime Minister SURAPHONG Towijakchaikun also spelled SURAPONG Tovichakchaikul (since 28 October 2012); Deputy Prime Minister YUKHON Limiaemthong (since 25 March 2013)

cabinet: Council of Ministers

note: there is also a Privy Council advising the king

elections: the monarchy is hereditary; according to the 2007 constitution, the prime minister is elected from among members of the House of Representatives; following national elections for the House of Representatives, the leader of the party positioned to organize a majority coalition usually becomes prime minister by appointment by the king; the prime minister is limited to two four-year terms

Legislative branch:

bicameral National Assembly or Rathasapha consisted of the Senate or Wuthisapha (150 seats; 77 members elected by popular vote representing 77 provinces, 73 appointed by judges and independent government bodies; members serve six-year terms) and the House of Representatives or Sapha Phuthaen Ratsadon (500 seats; 375 members elected from 375 single-seat constituencies and 125 elected on proportional party-list basis; members serve four-year terms)

elections: Senate - last held on 2 March 2008 (next to be held in March 2014); House of Representatives - last election held on 3 July 2011 (next to be held by July 2015)

election results: Senate - percent of vote by party - NA; seats by party - NA; House of Representatives - percent of vote by party - NA; seats by party - PTP 265, DP 159, PJT 34, CTP 19, others 23

note: 74 senators were appointed on 19 February 2008 by a seven-member committee headed by the chief of the Constitutional Court; 76 senators were elected on 2 March 2008; elections to the Senate are non-partisan; registered political party members are disqualified from being senators

Judicial branch:

highest court(s): Supreme Court of Justice (consists of the court president, 6 vice-presidents, and NA judges and organized into civil and criminal divisions); Constitutional Court (consists of the court president and 8 judges); Supreme Administrative Court (the number of judges determined by the Judicial Commission of the Administrative Courts)

judge selection and term of office: Supreme Court judges selected by the Judicial Commission of the Courts of Justice and approved by the monarch; judges' terms NA; Constitutional Court justices - 3 judges drawn from the Supreme Court, 2 judges drawn from the Administrative Court, and 4 judge candidates selected by the Selective Committee for Judges of the Constitutional Court and confirmed by the Senate; judges appointed by the monarch to serve single 9-year terms; Supreme Administrative Court judges selected by the Judicial Commission of the Administrative Courts and appointed by the monarch; judge tenure NA

subordinate courts: courts of first instance and appeals courts within both the judicial and administrative systems; military courts

Political parties and leaders:

Chat Pattana Party or CPN (Nation Development Party [WANNARAT Channukul]

Chat Thai Phattana Party or CTP (Thai Nation Development Party) [THAWORN Jampa-ngoen (acting)]

Mahachon Party or Mass Party [APHIRAT Sirinawin]

Matubhum Party (Motherland Party [SONTHI Bunyaratkalin])
Phalang Chon Party (People [Chonburi] Power Party) [CHAO Maneewong]
Phumjai (Bhumjai) Thai Party or PJT (Thai Pride) [ANUTIN Charnvirakul]
Prachathipat Party or DP (Democrat Party) [ABHISIT Wechachiwa, also spelled ABHISIT Vejjajiva]
Prachathipathai Mai Party (New Democrat Party) [SURATIN Phijarn]
Puea Thai Party (For Thais Party) or PTP [CHARUPHONG Rueangsusan also spelled JARUPONG Ruangsuwan]
Rak Prathet Thai Party (Love Thailand Party) [CHUWIT Kamonwisit]
Rak Santi Party (Peace Conservation Party) [THAWIL Surachetphong]

Political pressure groups and leaders:
Multicolor Group
People's Alliance for Democracy or PAD
United Front for Democracy Against Dictatorship or UDD

International organization participation:
ADB, APEC, ARF, ASEAN, BIMSTEC, BIS, CD, CICA, CP, EAS, FAO, G-77, IAEA, IBRD, ICAO, ICC (national committees), ICRM, IDA, IFAD, IFC, IFRCS, IHO, ILO, IMF, IMO, IMSO, Interpol, IOC, IOM, IPU, ISO, ITSO, ITU, ITUC (NGOs), MIGA, NAM, OAS (observer), OIC (observer), OIF (observer), OPCW, OSCE (partner), PCA, PIF (partner), UN, UNAMID, UNCTAD, UNESCO, UNHCR, UNIDO, UNMOGIP, UNWTO, UPU, WCO, WFTU (NGOs), WHO, WIPO, WMO, WTO

Diplomatic representation in the US:
chief of mission: Ambassador CHAIYONG Satchiphanon (also spelled CHAIYONG Satjipanon)
chancery: 1024 Wisconsin Avenue NW, Suite 401, Washington, DC 20007
telephone: [1] (202) 944-3600
FAX: [1] (202) 944-3611
consulate(s) general: Chicago, Los Angeles, New York

Diplomatic representation from the US:
chief of mission: Ambassador Kristie A. KENNEY
embassy: 120-122 Wireless Road, Bangkok 10330

mailing address: APO AP 96546
telephone: [66] (2) 205-4000
FAX: [66] (2) 254-2990, 205-4131
consulate(s) general: Chiang Mai

Key Leaders:

King	**PHUMIPHON Adunyadet**
Prime Min.	**YINGLAK Chinnawat**
Dep. Prime Min.	**KITTIRAT Na Ranong**
Dep. Prime Min.	**PHONGTHEP Thepkanchana**
Dep. Prime Min.	**PLODPRASOP Surasawadi**
Dep. Prime Min.	**PRACHA Promnok**
Dep. Prime Min.	**SURAPHONG Towijakchaikun**
Dep. Prime Min.	**YUKHON Limlaemthong**
Min. to the Prime Min.'s Office	**NIWATTHAMRONG Bunsongphaisan**
Min. to the Prime Min.'s Office	**SANTI Prompat**
Min. to the Prime Min.'s Office	**WARATHEP Ratthanakon**
Min. of Agriculture & Cooperatives	**YUKHON Limlaemthong**
Min. of Commerce	**NIWATTHAMRONG Bunsongphaisan**
Min. of Culture	**SONTHAYA Khunploem**
Min. of Defense	**YINGLAK Chinnawat**
Min. of Education	**CHATURON Chaisaeng**
Min. of Energy	**PHONGSAK**

	Raktaphongphaisan
Min. of Finance	**KITTIRAT Na Ranong**
Min. of Foreign Affairs	**SURAPHONG Towijakchaikun**
Min. of Industry	**PRASERT Boonchaisuk**
Min. of Information & Communications Technology	**ANUDIT Nakhonthap**
Min. of Interior	**CHARUPHONG Rueangsuwan**
Min. of Justice	**CHAIKASEM Nitisiri**
Min. of Labor	**CHALERM Yoobamrung**
Min. of Natural Resources & Environment	**WICHET Kasemthongsri**
Min. of Public Health	**PRADIT Sinthawanarong**
Min. of Science & Technology	**PEERAPHAN Palusuk**
Min. of Social Development & Human Security	**PAVEENA Hongsakun**
Min. of Tourism & Sports	**SOMSAK Phurisak**
Min. of Transport	**CHADCHAT Sitthiphan**
Governor, Bank of Thailand	**PRASAN Trairatworakun**
Ambassador to the US	**CHAIYONG Satchiphanon**
Permanent	**NORACHIT Sinhaseni**

| Representative to the UN, New York | |

Flag description:
> five horizontal bands of red (top), white, blue (double width), white, and red; the red color symbolizes the nation and the blood of life; white represents religion and the purity of Buddhism; blue stands for the monarchy
>
> note: similar to the flag of Costa Rica but with the blue and red colors reversed

National symbol(s):
> garuda (mythical half-man, half-bird figure); elephant

National anthem:
> name: "Phleng Chat Thai" (National Anthem of Thailand)
>
> lyrics/music: Luang SARANUPRAPAN/Phra JENDURIYANG
>
> note: music adopted 1932, lyrics adopted 1939; by law, people are required to stand for the national anthem at 0800 and 1800 every day; the anthem is played in schools, offices, theaters, and on television and radio during this time; "Phleng Sansasoen Phra Barami" (A Salute to the Monarch) serves as the royal anthem and is played in the presence of the royal family and during certain state ceremonies

Chapter 5: Economy

Economy - overview:

With a well-developed infrastructure, a free-enterprise economy, generally pro-investment policies, and strong export industries, Thailand achieved steady growth due largely to industrial and agriculture exports - mostly electronics, agricultural commodities, automobiles and parts, and processed foods. Thailand is trying to maintain growth by encouraging domestic consumption and public investment to offset weak exports in 2012. Unemployment, at less than 1% of the labor force, stands as one of the lowest levels in the world, which puts upward pressure on wages in some industries. Thailand also attracts nearly 2.5 million migrant workers from neighboring countries. The Thai government is implementing a nation-wide 300 baht ($10) per day minimum wage policy and deploying new tax reforms designed to lower rates on middle-income earners. The Thai economy has weathered internal and external economic shocks in recent years. The global economic severely cut Thailand's exports, with most sectors experiencing double-digit drops. In 2009, the economy contracted 2.3%. However, in 2010, Thailand's economy expanded 7.8%, its fastest pace since 1995, as exports rebounded. In late 2011 growth was interrupted by historic flooding in the industrial areas in Bangkok and its five surrounding provinces, crippling the manufacturing sector. Industry recovered from the second quarter of 2012 onward with GDP growth at 5.5% in 2012. The government has approved flood mitigation projects worth $11.7 billion, which were started in 2012, to prevent similar economic damage, and an additional $75 billion for infrastructure over the next seven years with a plan to start in 2013.

GDP (purchasing power parity):

$662.6 billion (2012 est.)

country comparison to the world: 25

$622.5 billion (2011 est.)

$622 billion (2010 est.)

note: data are in 2012 US dollars

GDP (official exchange rate):

$365.6 billion (2012 est.)

GDP - real growth rate:
>6.4% (2012 est.)
>
>country comparison to the world: 39
>
>0.1% (2011 est.)
>
>7.8% (2010 est.)

GDP - per capita (PPP):
>$10,300 (2012 est.)
>
>country comparison to the world: 116
>
>$9,700 (2011 est.)
>
>$9,700 (2010 est.)
>
>note: data are in 2012 US dollars

GDP - composition by sector:
>agriculture: 12.3%
>
>industry: 43.6%
>
>services: 44.2% (2012 est.)

Labor force:
>39.41 million (2012 est.)
>
>country comparison to the world: 17

Labor force - by occupation:
>agriculture: 38.2%
>
>industry: 13.6%
>
>services: 48.2% (2011 est.)

Unemployment rate:
>0.7% (2012 est.)
>
>country comparison to the world: 4
>
>0.7% (2011 est.)

Population below poverty line:
>7.8% (2010 est.)

Household income or consumption by percentage share:
>lowest 10%: 2.8%
>
>highest 10%: 31.5% (2009 est.)

Distribution of family income - Gini index:
> 53.6 (2009)
> country comparison to the world: 12
> 42 (2002)

Investment (gross fixed):
> 28.5% of GDP (2012 est.)
> country comparison to the world: 29

Budget:
> revenues: $71.4 billion
> expenditures: $88.03 billion (2012 est.)

Taxes and other revenues:
> 19.5% of GDP (2012 est.)
> country comparison to the world: 169

Budget surplus (+) or deficit (-):
> -4.6% of GDP (2012 est.)
> country comparison to the world: 161

Public debt:
> 44.5% of GDP (2012 est.)
> country comparison to the world: 77
> 40.3% of GDP (2011 est.)
> note: data cover general government debt, and includes debt instruments issued (or owned) by government entities other than the treasury; the data include treasury debt held by foreign entities; the data include debt issued by subnational entities, as well as intra-governmental debt; intra-governmental debt consists of treasury borrowings from surpluses in the social funds, such as for retirement, medical care, and unemployment; debt instruments for the social funds are sold at public auctions

Inflation rate (consumer prices):
> 3% (2012 est.)
> country comparison to the world: 93
> 3.8% (2011 est.)

Central bank discount rate:

2.75% (31 December 2012 est.)

country comparison to the world: 101

3.25% (31 December 2011 est.)

Commercial bank prime lending rate:

7.1% (31 December 2012 est.)

country comparison to the world: 127

6.91% (31 December 2011 est.)

Stock of narrow money:

$52.18 billion (31 December 2012 est.)

country comparison to the world: 46

$44.63 billion (31 December 2011 est.)

Stock of broad money:

$488.7 billion (31 December 2012 est.)

country comparison to the world: 22

$429.8 billion (31 December 2011 est.)

Stock of domestic credit:

$480.5 billion (31 December 2012 est.)

country comparison to the world: 26

$403.3 billion (31 December 2011 est.)

Market value of publicly traded shares:

$245 billion (31 December 2012)

country comparison to the world: 32

$230.9 billion (31 December 2011)

$218.7 billion (31 December 2010)

Agriculture - products:

rice, cassava (manioc), rubber, corn, sugarcane, coconuts, soybeans

Industries:

tourism, textiles and garments, agricultural processing, beverages, tobacco, cement, light manufacturing such as jewelry and electric appliances, computers and parts, integrated circuits, furniture, plastics, automobiles and automotive parts; world's second-largest tungsten producer and third-largest tin producer

Industrial production growth rate:
>7.2% (2012 est.)
>
>country comparison to the world: 25

Current account balance:
>-$2.728 billion (2012 est.)
>
>country comparison to the world: 147
>
>$5.889 billion (2011 est.)

Exports:
>$226.2 billion (2012 est.)
>
>country comparison to the world: 26
>
>$219.1 billion (2011 est.)

Exports - commodities:
>electronics, computer parts, automobiles and parts, electrical appliances, machinery and equipment, textiles and footwear, fishery products, rice, rubber

Exports - partners:
>China 11.7%, Japan 10.2%, US 9.9%, Hong Kong 5.7%, Malaysia 5.4%, Indonesia 4.9%, Singapore 4.7%, Australia 4.3% (2012)

Imports:
>$217.8 billion (2012 est.)
>
>country comparison to the world: 25
>
>$202.1 billion (2011 est.)

Imports - commodities:
>capital goods, intermediate goods and raw materials, consumer goods, fuels

Imports - partners:
>Japan 20%, China 14.9%, UAE 6.3%, Malaysia 5.3%, US 5.3% (2012)

Reserves of foreign exchange and gold:
>$181.6 billion (31 December 2012 est.)
>
>country comparison to the world: 17
>
>$175.1 billion (31 December 2011 est.)

Debt - external:
>$133.7 billion (31 December 2012 est.)

country comparison to the world: 42

$104.6 billion (31 December 2011 est.)

Stock of direct foreign investment - at home:

$159.1 billion (31 December 2012 est.)

country comparison to the world: 28

$150.5 billion (31 December 2011 est.)

Stock of direct foreign investment - abroad:

$51.59 billion (31 December 2012 est.)

country comparison to the world: 37

$40.65 billion (31 December 2011 est.)

Exchange rates:

baht per US dollar:

31.083 (2012 est.)

30.492 (2011 est.)

31.686 (2010 est.)

34.286 (2009)

33.37 (2008)

Fiscal year:

1 October - 30 September

Chapter 6: Energy

Electricity - production:
>173.3 billion kWh (2012 est.)
>
>country comparison to the world: 25

Electricity - consumption:
>169.4 billion kWh (2012 est.)
>
>country comparison to the world: 23

Electricity - exports:
>1.535 billion kWh (2012 est.)
>
>country comparison to the world: 47

Electricity - imports:
>9.575 billion kWh (2012 est.)
>
>country comparison to the world: 24

Electricity - installed generating capacity:
>32.6 million kW (2012 est.)
>
>country comparison to the world: 26

Electricity - from fossil fuels:
>89% of total installed capacity (2012 est.)
>
>country comparison to the world: 77

Electricity - from nuclear fuels:
>0% of total installed capacity (2012 est.)
>
>country comparison to the world: 183

Electricity - from hydroelectric plants:
>10.9% of total installed capacity (2012 est.)
>
>country comparison to the world: 114

Electricity - from other renewable sources:
>0.2% of total installed capacity (2012 est.)
>
>country comparison to the world: 88

Crude oil - production:
>213,000 bbl/day (2011 est.)

country comparison to the world: 40

Crude oil - exports:

32,200 bbl/day (2011 est.)

country comparison to the world: 51

Crude oil - imports:

793,900 bbl/day (2011 est.)

country comparison to the world: 15

Crude oil - proved reserves:

442 million bbl (1 January 2012 est.)

country comparison to the world: 53

Refined petroleum products - production:

913,600 bbl/day (2011 est.)

country comparison to the world: 24

Refined petroleum products - consumption:

721,100 bbl/day (2011 est.)

country comparison to the world: 26

Refined petroleum products - exports:

192,400 bbl/day (2011 est.)

country comparison to the world: 34

Refined petroleum products - imports:

41,700 bbl/day (2011 est.)

country comparison to the world: 74

Natural gas - production:

28.21 billion cu m (2011 est.)

country comparison to the world: 31

Natural gas - consumption:

45.08 billion cu m (2010 est.)

country comparison to the world: 21

Natural gas - exports:

0 cu m (2010 est.)

country comparison to the world: 187

Natural gas - imports:
 8.81 billion cu m (2010 est.)
 country comparison to the world: 27

Natural gas - proved reserves:
 299.8 billion cu m (1 January 2012 est.)
 country comparison to the world: 40

Carbon dioxide emissions from consumption of energy:
 278.5 million Mt (2010 est.)
 country comparison to the world: 22

Chapter 7: Communications

Telephones - main lines in use:
>   6.661 million (2011)
>   country comparison to the world: 28

Telephones - mobile cellular:
>   77.605 million (2011)
>   country comparison to the world: 18

Telephone system:
>   general assessment: high quality system, especially in urban areas like Bangkok
>   domestic: fixed line system provided by both a government-owned and commercial provider; wireless service expanding rapidly
>   international: country code - 66; connected to major submarine cable systems providing links throughout Asia, Australia, Middle East, Europe, and US; satellite earth stations - 2 Intelsat (1 Indian Ocean, 1 Pacific Ocean) (2011)

Broadcast media:
>   6 terrestrial TV stations in Bangkok broadcast nationally via relay stations - 2 of the networks are owned by the military, the other 4 are government-owned or controlled, leased to private enterprise, and all are required to broadcast government-produced news programs twice a day; multi-channel satellite and cable TV subscription services are available; radio frequencies have been allotted for more than 500 government and commercial radio stations; many small community radio stations operate with low-power transmitters (2008)

Internet country code:
>   .th

Internet hosts:
>   3.399 million (2012)
>   country comparison to the world: 31

Internet users:
>   17.483 million (2009)
>   country comparison to the world: 23

Chapter 8: Transportation

Airports:
>103 (2012)
>country comparison to the world: 55

Airports - with paved runways:
>total: 63
>over 3,047 m: 8
>2,438 to 3,047 m: 12
>1,524 to 2,437 m: 23
>914 to 1,523 m: 15
>under 914 m: 5 (2012)

Airports - with unpaved runways:
>total: 40
>1,524 to 2,437 m: 1
>914 to 1,523 m: 12
>under 914 m: 27 (2012)

Heliports:
>6 (2012)

Pipelines:
>condensate 2 km; gas 5,900 km; liquid petroleum gas 85 km; oil 1 km; refined products 1,097 km (2013)

Railways:
>total: 4,071 km
>country comparison to the world: 42
>standard gauge: 29 km 1.435-m gauge (29 km electrified)
>narrow gauge: 4,042 km 1.000-m gauge (2008)

Roadways:
>total: 180,053 km (includes 450 km of expressways) (2006)
>country comparison to the world: 27

Waterways:

4,000 km (3,701 km navigable by boats with drafts up to 0.9 m) (2011)

country comparison to the world: 26

Merchant marine:

total: 363

country comparison to the world: 28

by type: bulk carrier 31, cargo 99, chemical tanker 28, container 18, liquefied gas 36, passenger 1, passenger/cargo 10, petroleum tanker 114, refrigerated cargo 24, roll on/roll off 1, vehicle carrier 1

foreign-owned: 13 (China 1, Hong Kong 1, Malaysia 3, Singapore 1, Taiwan 1, UK 6)

registered in other countries: 46 (Bahamas 4, Belize 1, Honduras 2, Panama 6, Singapore 33) (2010)

Ports and terminals:

Bangkok, Laem Chabang, Map Ta Phut, Prachuap Port, Si Racha

Chapter 9: Military

Military branches:
> Royal Thai Army (Kongthap Bok Thai, RTA), Royal Thai Navy (Kongthap Ruea Thai, RTN, includes Royal Thai Marine Corps), Royal Thai Air Force (Kongthap Agard Thai, RTAF) (2013)

Military service age and obligation:
> 21 years of age for compulsory military service; 18 years of age for voluntary military service; males register at 18 years of age; 2-year conscript service obligation (2012)

Manpower available for military service:
> males age 16-49: 17,689,921
>
> females age 16-49: 17,754,795 (2010 est.)

Manpower fit for military service:
> males age 16-49: 13,308,372
>
> females age 16-49: 14,182,567 (2010 est.)

Manpower reaching militarily significant age annually:
> male: 533,424
>
> female: 509,780 (2010 est.)

Military expenditures:
> 1.8% of GDP (2005 est.)
>
> country comparison to the world: 81

Chapter 10: Transnational Issues

Disputes - international:

    separatist violence in Thailand's predominantly Malay-Muslim southern provinces prompt border closures and controls with Malaysia to stem insurgent activities; Southeast Asian states have enhanced border surveillance to check the spread of avian flu; talks continue on completion of demarcation with Laos but disputes remain over several islands in the Mekong River; despite continuing border committee talks, Thailand must deal with Karen and other ethnic rebels, refugees, and illegal cross-border activities; Cambodia and Thailand dispute sections of boundary; in 2011 Thailand and Cambodia resorted to arms in the dispute over the location of the boundary on the precipice surmounted by Preah Vihear temple ruins, awarded to Cambodia by ICJ decision in 1962 and part of a planned UN World Heritage site; Thailand is studying the feasibility of jointly constructing the Hatgyi Dam on the Salween river near the border with Burma; in 2004, international environmentalist pressure prompted China to halt construction of 13 dams on the Salween River that flows through China, Burma, and Thailand; 140,000 mostly Karen refugees fleeing civil strife, political upheaval and economic stagnation in Burma live in remote camps in Thailand near the border

Refugees and internally displaced persons:

    refugees (country of origin): 88,148 (Burma) (2011)

    IDPs: undetermined (resurgence in ethno-nationalist violence in south of country since 2004)(2011)

Illicit drugs:

    a minor producer of opium, heroin, and marijuana; transit point for illicit heroin en route to the international drug market from Burma and Laos; eradication efforts have reduced the area of cannabis cultivation and shifted some production to neighboring countries; opium poppy cultivation has been reduced by eradication efforts; also a drug money-laundering center; minor role in methamphetamine production for regional consumption; major consumer of methamphetamine since the 1990s despite a series of government crackdowns

Map of Thailand

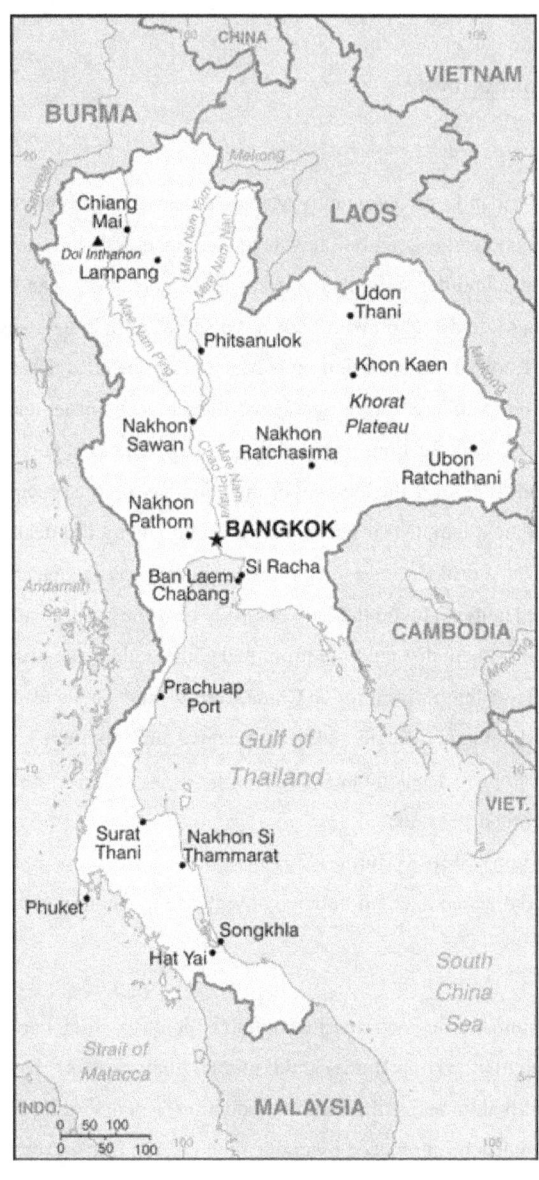

Other Key Facts™ Titles

Key Facts on Syria

Key Facts on China

Key Facts on Qatar

Key Facts on India

Key Facts on Germany

Key Facts on Argentina

Key Facts on Russia

Key Facts on North Korea

Key Facts on Brazil

Key Facts on Italy

Key Facts on the United Arab Emirates

Key Facts on the European Union

Key Facts on Pakistan

Key Facts on Saudi Arabia

Key Facts on Cyprus

Key Facts on Iran

Key Facts on Afghanistan

Key Facts on Iraq

Key Facts on Indonesia

Key Facts on South Korea

Key Facts on France

Key Facts on the United Kingdom

Key Facts on Egypt

Key Facts on Israel

Key Facts on Mexico

Key Facts on the United States of America

Key Facts on Turkey

Key Facts on South Africa

Key Facts on Greece

Key Facts on Japan

Key Facts on Malaysia

Key Facts on Vietnam

Key Facts on Hong Kong

Key Facts on Jordan

Key Facts on Australia

Key Facts on Venezuela

Key Facts on Canada

Key Facts on Burma (Myanmar)

Key Facts on Myanmar (Burma)

Key Facts on Singapore

Key Facts on Ireland

Key Facts on The Philippines

All Key Facts™ Titles are Available at www.Amazon.com

THE INTERNATIONALIST®
2013
WWW.INTERNATIONALIST.COM

www.ingramcontent.com/pod-product-compliance
Lightning Source LLC
Chambersburg PA
CBHW070725180526
45167CB00004B/1616